SAUL AND DAVID

SAUL AND DAVID

A PLAY IN FIVE ACTS

by

VOLTAIRE

Adapted and Translated by Frank J. Morlock

THE BORGO PRESS

An Imprint of Wildside Press LLC

MMX

CONTENTS

DEDICATION

To

AL SEGAL

CAST OF CHARACTERS

Saul, son of Cis, first Jewish King.

David, son of Jesse, son-in-law of Saul, second Jewish King.

Agag, King of Amalecites

Samuel, Prophet and Judge of Israel.

Michol, wife of David and daughter of Saul

Abigail, widow of Nabal and second spouse of David

Bethsheba, wife of Uriah and concubine of

David.

Sybil (Pythoness) famous witch of Israel

Baza: long time confidant of Saul

Abiezer, a long time officer of Saul

Adoness, son of David and Agitha his seventeenth wife

Salomon, adulterous son of David and Bethsheba

Nathan, prince and prophet of Israel.

Gag or Gad, prophet and chaplain to David

Abesag of Suram, young Sunamite

Ebind, David's Captain.

Yesez, Inspector General of David's troops.

Priests of Saul

The Captains of David

A Clerk of the Treasury

A Messenger

The Jewish Population

ACT I

GALGA

BAZA: O great Saul! most potent of kings, you who reign over the three lakes, in the space of more than 500 stadia, you, conqueror of generous Agag, King of Alamec, whose captains were mounted on the most powerful donkeys, as well as the 500 sons of Alamec, you who Adonoi made triumph over Dagon and Beelzebub at the same time, you, who, no doubt, will place under your rule the entire earth, as was promised you so many times: must you abandon yourself to sorrow amidst such noble triumphs and such great hopes?

SAUL: O my dear Baza! A thousand times happier is he who leads in peace the sheep of Benjamin, and presses the sweet grapes of the valley of Enguddi! Alas, as I was seeking my father's she-asses, I found a kingdom; since that day I've known only sorrow. Had it pleased God, on the contrary, I ought to have sought a kingdom and found donkeys! I'd have made a better bargain.

BAZA: Is it the prophet Samuel? Is it your son-in-law David who causes you this mortal pain?

SAUL: The one and the other. Samuel, you know, anointed me despite himself. He did what he could to prevent the people from choosing a prince and once I was elected, he became the cruelest of my enemies.

BAZA: Actually, you ought to have expected it; he was a priest and you were a warrior; he governed before you, they always hate their successor.

SAUL: Eh! Could he hope to govern much longer? He's associated his unworthy children in his powers, equally corrupted and corrupters, who betrayed public justice; the whole nation rose against this sacerdotal government. They drew a king by lot. The sacred dice announced the will of heaven, the people ratified it—and Samuel shivered: It's not enough to hate in me a prince chosen by heaven, he hates even the prophet, because he knows that, like him, I have the name of a clairvoyant, that I have prophesied like him, and this new proverb spreads through Israel "Saul is also of the rank of the prophets" offending only his over-proud ears; he's still respected; to my misfortune he's a priest, he's dangerous.

BAZA: Is it not he who is raising your son-in-law David against you?

SAUL: That's only too true, and I tremble that he's conspiring to give my crown to this rebel.

BAZA: Your Royal Highness is too well strengthened by his victories, and King Agag, your illustrious prisoner. You are here a sure guaranty of the fidelity of your people, equally enchanted by your victory and your clemency. Here's someone they are bringing before Your Royal Highness.

(Enter Agag and soldiers)

AGAG: Gentle and powerful conqueror, model of princes who knows how to vanquish and pardon, I cast myself at your sacred knees. Deign to set what I must give as my ransom yourself. Henceforth, I will be your neighbor a faithful ally, a submissive vassal, and I will see in you only a benefactor and master; I owe you my life, in addition, I shall owe you my freedom. I will admire, I will love in you the image of God who punishes and forgives.

SAUL: Illustrious prince, were the misfortunes yet greater, I did only my duty in saving your life; kings owe respect to their own kind. He who takes vengeance after victory is unworthy of conquering. I am not setting a ransom on your person, it is of inestimable worth. You are free. The tribute that you will pay to Israel will be less marks of submission than of friendship. This is how kings ought to deal with each other.

AGAG: O virtue! O grandeur of courage! How much power you have in my heart! I will live, I will die, the subject of great Saul, and all my estates are his.

(Enter Samuel and priests.)

SAUL: Samuel, what news do you bring me? Do you come on behalf of God, the people, or on your own?

SAMUEL: On behalf of God.

SAUL: What does he order?

SAMUEL: He directs me to tell you that he repents of having made you reign.

SAUL: God repents of it! Only those who have committed sin repent; his eternal wisdom cannot be imprudent. God cannot commit sin.

SAMUEL: He can repent of having placed on the throne those who are committing them.

SAUL: Well, what man doesn't commit them? Of what am I guilty?

SAMUEL: Of having pardoned a king.

AGAG: What! The most beautiful of virtues would be regarded by you as a crime?

SAMUEL: (to Agag) Shut up, don't blaspheme further!

(to Saul) Saul, formerly King of Jews, didn't God order you through my mouth to cut the throat of all the Amalects without sparing either the women, the young girls, nor the infants at the breast.

AGAG: Your God ordered you to do this! You are mistaken, you meant to say the devil.

SAUL: (to his priests) Prepare to obey me; and you Saul, have you obeyed God?

SAUL: I didn't believe that such an order was positive; I thought that bounty was the premier attribute of the Supreme Being, that a compassionate heart could never displease him.

SAMUEL: You deceived yourself, unfaithful man; God condemns you, your scepter will pass into other hands.

BAZA: (to Saul) What insolence! Lord, allow me to punish this barbarous priest.

SAUL: Be very careful of doing that; don't you see he is followed by all the people and that we would be stoned to death if I resisted, for indeed, I had promised.

BAZA: You promised an abominable thing!

SAUL: Never mind; the Jews are still more abominable; they will defend Samuel against me.

BAZA: Ah, unlucky prince! You have courage only at the head of armies.

SAUL: Well then, in that case! Priest, what must I do?

SAMUEL: I am going to show you how to obey the Lord. (to his priests) O sacred priests! Children of Lax, deploy your zeal here; let them bring a table; let them stretch this king on that table, whose foreskin is a crime before the Lord.

(The priests chain Agag on a table)

AGAG: What do you want from me? Pitiless monsters!

SAUL: August Samuel in the name of the Lord!

SAMUEL: Don't invoke him, you are unworthy of him; stay here, he orders you to be witness to the sacrifice, which may expiate your crime.

AGAG: (to Samuel) So thus you are going to

give me death? O death, how bitter you are!

SAMUEL: Yes, you are fat, and your holocaust will be more agreeable to the Lord.

AGAG: Alas! Saul, how I pity you for being submissive to such monsters!

SAMUEL: (to Agag) Listen, you are going to die; do you want to be Jewish? Do you want to be circumcised?

AGAG: And if I were so weak as to be of your religion, would you give me life?

SAMUEL: No, you will have the satisfaction of dying Jewish and that's quite enough.

AGAG: In that case, strike, executioner!

SAMUEL: Give me that ax in the name of the Lord, and while I cut an arm, you cut a leg, and thus from one bit by bit.

(They all strike together in the name of the Lord)

AGAG: O death! O torture! O barbarians!

SAUL: Must I be witness to so horrible an abomination?

BAZA: God will punish you for having suffered it.

SAMUEL: (to priests) Take away this body and this table. Let the remains of this infidel be burned, and let his flesh serve to nourish our servants. (to Saul) And you, prince, learn that at all times obedience is worth more than sacrifice.

SAUL: (hurling himself into a chair) I am dying, I cannot survive so many horrors and so much shame.

(Samuel leaves with priests)

MESSENGER: (entering) Lord: think of your safety; David is approaching in arms, he is followed by 500 brigands that he's gathered; you have only a weak guard.

BAZA: Well! Lord, you see: David and Samuel were in cahoots, you are betrayed on all sides. But I shall be faithful to you until death! What role will you take?

SAUL: That of battle and death.

CURTAIN

ACT II

ON THE HILL OF ACHILA

MICHOL: Pitiless spouse, do you pretend to attempt the life of my father, of your benefactor, of the one who, having first taken you for his harp player, soon after made you his shield bearer, who finally placed you in my arms?

DAVID: It's true, my dear Michol, that I owe him the joy of possessing your charms; it cost me dear enough; I had to bring to your father the foreskins of 200 Philistines; I was obliged to kill 200 men to come to the end of that enterprise, and I didn't have the jaw of Samson's ass; but were it necessary to battle all the forces of Egypt and Babylon, I would have done it to deserve you; I adored you and I adore you.

MICHOL: And to prove your love you want the life of my father.

DAVID: God preserve me from it! I only wish to succeed him: you know that I've respected his life and that when I met him in a cavern I cut only the tip of his cloak; the life of the father of my dear Michol will always be precious to me.

MICHOL: Why then are you joining his enemies? Why are you soiling yourself with the horrible crime of rebellion, and rendering yourself thereby so unworthy of the throne to which you aspire? Why on one side are you joining with Samuel our domestic enemy, and on the other with Akis, King of Geth our declared enemy?

DAVID: My noble spouse, don't condemn me without listening to me, you know that one day in the village of Bethlehem Samuel poured oil on my head, thus I am king, and you are the wife of a king. If I am joining myself to the enemies of the nation, if I've done ill to my fellow citizens, I've done more to those same enemies. It's true that I've engaged my faith to the King of Geth, generous Akis; I've assembled 500 malefactors ruined with debts and debauchery, but good soldiers all. Akis received us, and heaped benefits on me, he treated me like a son: he has complete confidence in me but I've never forgotten that I am Jewish, and having commissions from King Akis to go ravage your territories I've very often ravaged his; I went into the most distant villages and killed all without mercy, I pardoned neither sex nor age, so as to be pure before the Lord and so there shall not be found any to betray me to King Akis. I brought to him cattle, asses, sheep, the she-goats of innocent farmers that I'd slaughtered, and I told him with a salutary lie that they were the cattle, asses, sheep, and she-goats of Jews. When I met some resistance I would saw in two the best body of the insolent rebels, or I would crush them under the teeth of their portcullis or I would roast them in brick ovens. See if that's love of country, if that's being a good Israelite.

MICHOL: Thus, cruel one, you've equally shed the blood of your brothers and those of your allies' you've betrayed equally these two benefactors, nothing is sacred to you. You will betray your dear Michol who burns for you with such an unhappy love.

DAVID: No, I swear by the Rod of Aaron, by

the root of Jesse, I will always be faithful to you.

(Enter Abigail)

ABIGAIL: (embracing David) My dear, my
tender spouse, master of my heart and
life, come, leave these dangerous parts
with me; Saul is arming himself against
you, and Akis is expecting you.

MICHOL: What do I hear? Her spouse?
What! Perfidious monster you swore to
me an eternal love and you've taken another wife! Who is this insolent rival?

DAVID: I am confounded.

ABIGAIL: August and amicable daughter of
a great king, don't get angry with your
servant. A hero like David has need of
several wives, and as for me, I'm a
young widow in need of a husband. You
are obliged to be always near your fa-

ther, the King. David must have a companion in his travels and in his work; don't envy me this honor. I will always be submissive to you.

MICHOL: At least she's civil and gracious, not like those impertinent concubines that are always braving the mistress of the house; monster, where did you make this acquaintance?

DAVID: Since the truth must be told, my dear Michol, I was at the head of my brigands and exercising the right of war, I ordered Nabal, the husband of Abigail to bring me all he had; Nabal was a brute who didn't know the customs of the world, he insolently refused me; Abigail was born, gentle, honest, and tender. She stole all that she could from her husband to bring me: at the end of a week the brute was dead.

MICHOL: I suspected as much.

DAVID: And I married the widow!

MICHOL: So, Abigail is my equal; indeed, tell me, in conscience, very dear brigand—how many wives have you got?

DAVID: I have only eighteen counting you: that's not too many for a brave man.

MICHOL: Eighteen wives, rogue. Eh! What are you doing then, with all that?

DAVID: I give what I can of all that I've pillaged.

MICHOL: See how well they are supported! You are like birds of prey who bring pigeons to their females to devour. Yet they have only one companion and the son of Jesse must have eighteen!

DAVID: My dear Michol, you will never notice that you have companions.

MICHOL: Go, you make more promises than you can keep. Although you have eighteen, I forgive you; if I had only one rival I would be more difficult; still, you will pay me for it.

ABIGAIL: August Queen, if all the rest thought like me, you would have seventeen more slaves around you.

ABEAR (entering) My master, what are you doing here between the women? Saul advances from the West, and Akis from the orient; which side will you march?

DAVID: On the side of Akis, without hesitation.

MICHOL: What! Wretch, against your king! Against my father!

DAVID: Indeed, it's necessary; there's more to be gained with Akis than with Saul; console yourself, Michol; goodbye,

Abigail

ABIGAIL: No, I won't leave you.

DAVID: Remain, I tell you; this is not a woman's business; everything has its time, I am going to fight: pray God for me!

(Exit David)

ABIGAIL: Protect me noble daughter of Saul; I think such an action worthy of your great heart. David has just espoused a new wife this morning; let us join together against our rivals.

MICHOL: What! This very morning! And what's her name.

ABIGAIL: Alichenoam, she's one of the most shameless hussies in the whole race of Jacob.

MICHOL: It's a villainous race, this race of Jacob: but by God, since my husband treats us so unworthily, I will treat him the same. And I am going to do it by marrying another.

ABIGAIL: Go, go, Madame. I promise you to do as much when I am displeased with him.

(Enter Ebend, the Messenger)

EBEND: Ah, Princess! Your Jonathas, do you know?

MICHOL What then? My brother Jonathas?

EBEND: Is condemned to death, sacrificed to the Lord, anathematized.

ABIGAIL: Jonathas who loved your husband so much.

MICHOL: He's no more? They took his life

from him?

EBEND: No, Madame, he's in perfect health: the King, your father, marching at break of day against Akis, met a small band of Philistines, and as we were ten to one, we got the best of it, with courage. Saul, to augment the strength of a soldier was fasting, ordering that no one eat during the day, and swore he would sacrifice to the Lord the first to lunch: Jonathas who was unaware of this prudent order, had found a honeycomb and swallowed the length of my thumb. Saul rightly condemned him to die; he knew what it would cost him to fail in his word. The adventure with Agag terrified him; he feared Samuel, so in the end Jonathas was going to be offered as a victim. The whole army rose against the parricide; Jonathas was rescued, and the army set to eating and drinking, and, instead of losing Jonathas, we were defeated by Samuel. He died of apoplexy

MICHOL: So much the better; he was a villainous man.

ABIGAIL: God be blessed.

EBEND: King Saul is following all of his; I think he's going to hold a council in this hemp-field to know what to do to attack Akis and the Philistines.

MICHOL: (to Saul, Baza and Captains who enter) Father, must I tremble every day for your life, for that of my brothers and must I wipe off the infidelities of my husband?

SAUL: Your brother and your husband are rebels. What: eat honey on a day of battle! He's lucky that the army took his side; but your husband is a hundred times worse than he; I swear that I will treat him as Samuel treated Agag.

ABIGAIL: (to Michol) Ah, Madame, how

he's rolling his eyes, as if gnashing his teeth. Let's flee as fast as possible; your father is mad or I am much deceived,

MICHOL: Sometimes he's possessed by the devil.

SAUL: Daughter, who's this jade?

MICHOL: She's one of the wives of your son-in-law David that you used to love so much.

SAUL: She's pretty enough: I will take her myself on leaving the fort.

ABIGAIL: Ah! Nasty man! It's plain to see he's rejected.

MICHOL: Father, I see your illness has taken you. If David was here he would play the harp for you, because you know the harp is a remedy against hypochondriac vapors.

SAUL: Shut up, you are a dummy; I know better than you what I have to do.

ABIGAIL: Ah, Madame, how nasty he is! He's crazier than ever; let's withdraw as fast as possible.

MICHOL: It's that wretched butchery of Agag which has given him vapors, let's steal ourselves away from his fury.

(The women leave.)

SAUL: My captains go wait for me; Baza stay. You are seeing me in a moral fix; I have my vapors. It's necessary to do battle; we have powerful enemies, they are behind the mountain of Gelbon, I really want to know what will be the result of this battle.

BAZA: Eh, Lord! Nothing could be easier, Aren't you a prophet as much as another? Don't you even have vapors

which are a true forerunner of prophe-
cies?

SAUL: It's true, but for some time, the Lord no longer replies to me; I don't know what's wrong with me. Have you made the Pythoness of Endor come?

BAZA: Yes, my master. But do you believe the Lord will answer her, rather than you?

SAUL: Yes, no question for She has the mind of a Python.

BAZA: A mind of a python, Master; what species is that?

SAUL: My word, I don't know anything about it. But they say she's a very clever woman; I want to consult with the ghost of Samuel.

BAZA: You would do better to place yourself at the head of your troops. How does one consult a ghost?

SAUL: The pythoness makes them emerge from the ground, and you can see if their appearance is happy or sad.

BAZA: He's lost his mind! Don't in the name of God. Don't amass all these stupidities; and go put your troops in battle.

SAUL: Stay here; it's absolutely necessary that we see a shade. Now here's the Pythoness who's come: Protect yourself against letting me be recognized. She takes me for a captain.

PYTHONESS: (entering with a staff between her legs) What mortal wishes to snatch the secrets of the abyss that covers them? Which of the two of you addressed himself to me to know the future?

BAZA: (pointing to Saul) He's my captain. Shouldn't you know him since you are a sorceress?

PYTHONESS: (to Saul) So then it's for you that I am to force nature to interrupt the course of its eternal laws? How much will you give me?

SAUL: A crown. And you are paid in advance, old witch.

PYTHONESS: You will get your money's worth. The magicians of Pharoah, were, beside me, merely ignoramuses; they undertook to change the water of the Nile into blood. I shall do more, and first of all command the Sun to appear.

BAZA: At noon! What a miracle.

PYTHONESS: I see something on the ground.

SAUL: It's not a ghost.

PYTHONESS: Yes, a ghost.

SAUL: How does it look?

PYTHONESS: Like a shade.

SAUL: Does it have a huge beard?

PYTHONESS: Yes, a large cloak and a huge beard.

SAUL: A white beard?

PYTHONESS: White like snow.

SAUL: Exactly, it's the shade of Samuel; it must have a really nasty appearance.

PYTHONESS: Oh, they never change character. It's threatening you. It's making horrible eyes at you.

SAUL: Ah, I am lost.

BAZA: Eh, Lord! Can you amuse yourself with this insipidity? Don't you hear the sound of trumpets? The Philistines are approaching.

SAUL: Come on then; but he never hears me say anything good.

PYTHONESS: At least I have his money. Why, now there's a stupid captain.

CURTAIN

ACT III

SICELAG

DAVID (to his Captains) So then, Saul has killed my friends? His son Jonathas, too? And I am king of a small share of the country legitimately?

JOAB: Yes, indeed, Your Royal Highness did very well to hang the one who brought you news of Saul's death, for it is never permitted to say that a king is dead; that act of justice will conciliate all minds in your favor, it will be apparent that, at bottom, you loved your father-in-law, and that you are a good man.

DAVID: Yes; but Saul leaves children: Isobeth, his son already reigns over several tribes; what to do?

JOAB: Don't bother about it, I know two knaves who must assassinate Isobeth, if they haven't already done so; you will hang them both, and you will reign over Judah and Israel.

DAVID: Tell me a bit, the rest of you, Saul left a lot of money? Will I be quite rich?

ABIEZER: Alas, we don't have a penny; you know, two years ago, when Saul was elected king, we didn't have wherewithal to purchase weapons; there were only two sabers in the whole realm, yet they were all rusted; the Philistines whose slaves we had almost been, left us in our hovels only a scrap of iron to fix our ploughs, besides our ploughs were very useless in a bad stony land, bristling with bald mountains where there were only a few olives and few grapes; we had taken only cattle, goats and sheep from King Agag because that was all that he had. I don't think we could find ten crowns in all Judea; there were a few usurers who clipped cash in Tyre and Damascus but they would get themselves impaled rather than loan you a denarius.

DAVID: Has the little village of Salem and its castle been seized?

JOAB: Yes, milord.

ABIEZER: I am annoyed about it; that violence can discredit our new government. Salem belongs at all times to Jebuseesn, with whom we are not at war. It's a holy place because Melchesedech was once king of that village.

DAVID: There's no Melchesedech to hold it. I will make a fine fortress of it and I will call it Heru-Chalaim, this will be the place of my residence, our children will multiply like sand on the sea, and we will reign over the whole world.

JOAB: Eh, Lord, you cannot think it! This place is a sort of desert, where there are only stones for two leagues around. It lacks water; there's only a wretched little stream of Cedieu which is dry six months of the year. Rather why not go to the great highways towards Tyre, Damascus, Babylon; there would be great deeds to do.

DAVID: Yes, but all the peoples of those countries are powerful; we would risk getting ourselves hanged, finally the Lord has given me Heru-Chalaim. I shall dwell there, and I will praise the Lord.

A MESSENGER: (entering) Milord, two of your servants have just assassinated Isobeth, who had the insolence to want to succeed his father, and despite those on your side; they threw him out the window, he swam in his blood, the tribes that obeyed him have taken an oath to obey you, and they are bringing to you his sister Michol, your wife who you abandoned, and who just married Phatiel, son of Sais.

DAVID: They would have done better to leave her with him, what do they want me to do with that straight-laced woman? Go, my dear Joab, let them lock her up, go my friends, go seize all that Isobeth possessed, bring it to me, we will share it; You, Lord Joab, don't fail to hang those who delivered me from Isobeth, and who rendered me that signal service; all march before the Lord with confidence; I have some minor business that's a bit urgent; I will rejoin you in a short time to perform together actions of grace to the God of Arms who gave strength to my arm and who placed at my feet, the basilisk and the dragon.

ALL THE CAPTAINS: Huzza! Huzza! Long live David, our good King, the anointed of the Lord, the father of his people.

(They leave)

DAVID: (to servant) Show Bethsheba in,

(Bethsheba enters)

DAVID: My dear Bethsheba, I no longer love anyone but you: your teeth are like sheep emerging from a bath; your throat is like a bunch of grapes, your nose like the tower of Mount Liban; the kingdom that the Lord has given me is not worth one of your embraces; Michol, Abigail, and all my wives are worthy at most of being your servants.

BETHSHEBA: Alas, Milord, you were saying as much this morning to the young Abigail.

DAVID: It's true, she can please me for a moment, but you are my mistress at all hours, I will give you robes, cows, goats, sheep. As for money, I don't have any yet, but you shall once I've run my course on the great highways, be it towards the land of the Phoenicians, be it towards Damascus, be it towards Tyre. What's wrong, my dear Bethsheba? You're weeping.

BETHSHEBA: Alas, yes, Milord.

DAVID: Some one of my wives or concubines has mistreated you?

BETHSHEBA: No.

DAVID: What then is your shame?

BETHSHEBA: My Lord, I'm pregnant, my husband Uriah hasn't slept with me for a month and if he notices my pregnancy, I'm afraid of being beaten.

DAVID: Eh! Why didn't you make Uriah sleep with you?

BETHSHEBA: alas! I did what I could but he said he always wanted to stay close to you: you know he's fondly attached to you; he's one of the best officers in your army; he watches over your person while others sleep; he places himself in front of you while others drag their feet; if he gets some good booty he brings it to you; in short he prefers you to me.

DAVID: Now there's an unbearable pillar. Nothing is so odious as those eager folks who always want to render services without being asked: go, go, I will rid you of this importunate, give me a table and notebooks to write.

BETHSHEBA: Milord, for a table, you know there aren't any here; but here are my notebooks with a bodkin; you can write on my knees.

DAVID: Come, we'll write: Support of my crown, like me, servant of God, our loyal Uriah renders you this missive: march with him as soon as this present is received, against the body of Philistines who are at the other side of the valley of Hebron. Place the loyal Uriah in the first rank, abandon him as soon as the first arrow is shot, in a way so that he'll be killed by the enemy; and if he isn't struck in the front take care to have him assassinated in the rear; the whole thing being a work of state: God keep you in his holy protection. Your good King David.

BETHSHEBA: Eh! Good God! You want my poor husband killed?

DAVID: My dear child, these are little severities to which one is sometimes obliged to loan oneself; it's a small ill for a great good, solely in the intention of avoiding scandal.

BETHSHEBA: Alas, your servant has nothing to reply, let it be done according to your will.

DAVID: Let them call to me the good man Uriah.

BETHSHEBA: Alas! What do you wish to say to him? Will I be able to bear his presence?

DAVID: Don't trouble yourself. (to Uriah who enters) Here, my dear Uriah, bear this letter to my Captain Joab, and deserve forever the good graces of the Lord's anointed.

URIAH: I obey his commands with joy, my

feet, my arm, my life are at his service. I would die to prove my zeal to him.

DAVID: (embracing him) Your zeal will be fulfilled, my dear Uriah.

URIAH: Goodbye, my dear Bethsheba; be always attached, as I am to our master.

BETHSHEBA: That's what I'm doing, my dear husband.

DAVID: Dwell here, my beloved, I am obliged to give somewhat similar orders for the benefit of the realm; I'll come back to you in a moment.

BETHSHEBA: No, dear lover, I won't leave you.

DAVID: Ah! I really like women to be mistresses in bed: everywhere else I want them to be obedient.

CURTAIN

ACT IV

HEBRON

ABIGAIL: Bethsheba, Bethsheba, so this is the way you are stealing Milord's heart from me.

BETHSHEBA: You see I've stolen nothing from you since he's leaving me and I cannot stop him.

ABIGAIL: You stop him only too well, perfidious one, in the web of your wickedness. All Israel says you are pregnant by him.

BETHSHEBA: Well! Suppose so, Madame, is it for you to reproach me with it; didn't you do as much?

ABIGAIL: It's entirely different, Madame: I have the honor of being his spouse.

BETHSHEBA: Now there's a cute marriage. Everyone knows you poisoned Nabal, your husband, to marry David who was still only a captain.

ABIGAIL: No more reproaches, Madame, if you please. You would do quite as much to the good man Uriah to become Queen. But know that I am going to reveal all to him.

BETHSHEBA: I defy you to.

ABIGAIL: Meaning that the deed's already done.

BETHSHEBA: Whatever the case may be, I

shall be your queen and you will learn to respect me.

ABIGAIL: Me, respect you, Madame!

BETHSHEBA: Yes, madame!

ABIGAIL: Ah, Madame, Judea will produce wheat instead of rye, and it will have horses instead of donkeys to ride before I am reduced to such ignominy; it really becomes a woman like you to be impertinent to me!

BETHSHEBA: If I bethink myself, a pair of whacks—

ABIGAIL: Don't consider it, Madame, I have a good arm, and I'll rough you up in a way—

DAVID: (entering) Peace, will you, peace; are you mad, the rest of you? It is really a question of you quarreling like this when the horror of horrors is on my house.

BETHSHEBA: What is it, my dear lover! What's happened?

ABIGAIL: My dear husband, is there some new misfortune?

DAVID: See—didn't my son Ammon, whom you know, decide to rape his sister Thamor, and after that drive her from her room with big kicks in the ass.

ABIGAIL: What, that's all it is? I thought from your terrified appearance that someone had stolen your money.

DAVID: That's not all; my other son, Absalom, when he saw all this bickering set himself to kill Ammon; I got angry with my son Absalom; he's revolted against me, driven me from my town of Heru-Chalaim, and here I am in the street.

BETHSHEBA: Oh! These are really serious matters.

ABIGAIL: Villainous family, the family of David. Have you nothing, then, brigand? Your son is anointed in your place?

DAVID: Alas, yes, and for proof that he's anointed, he slept on the terrace of the fort with all my wives, one after the other!

ABIGAIL: O heavens! Why wasn't I there! I would much rather have slept with your son Absolam than with you, villainous robber that I am abandoning forever. He has hair which falls almost to his belt, and that he sells scraps of for 200 crowns per year at least; he's young, he's lovable, and you are only a debauched barbarian who mocks God, men, and women; go, I renounce you forever, and I'm giving myself to your son Absalom or to the first Philistine that I shall meet. (curtsying to Beth-sheba) Goodbye, Madame.

BETHSHEBA: Your servant, Madame.

DAVID: Now will you look at this Abigail that I thought was so sweet! Ah! Who-ever counts on a woman counts on the wind, and you my dear Bethsheba, will you abandon me, too?

BETHSHEBA: Alas, this is the way this sort of marriage ends. What do you expect to become of me if your son Absalom reigns? And if Uriah, my husband learns that you wanted to assassinate him, you will be ruined and me, too.

DAVID: Fear nothing; Uriah has been des-patched; my friend Joab is expeditious.

BETHSHEBA: What! My poor husband is assassinated! Hoo, hoo, hoo. (weeping) Ho, hee, ha.

DAVID: What! You are weeping for the good man?

BETHSHEBA: I can't prevent myself from doing it.

DAVID: Stupid things women are! They wish their husbands dead, they demand it, and once they've obtained it, they start crying.

BETHSHEBA: Forgive this little ceremony.

DAVID: (to Joab who enters) Well! Joab, what condition are things in. What's become of that rogue Absalom?

JOAB: By Sabath, I sent him with Uriah, I found him hanging from a tree by his hair and I bravely pierced him with three darts.

DAVID: Ah! Absalom my son! Hoo, hoo, hoo, hee, ho, hi.

BETHSHEBA: Now there you go crying for your son the way I was weeping for my husband. Everyone has their weakness.

DAVID: You cannot tame nature, some Jew may be able to, but it will pass, and the direction affairs are going in is proceeding quickly otherwise.

(The Prophet Nathan enters)

BETHSHEBA: Eh! There's Nathan the seer! God forgive me! What's he come here to do?

NATHAN: Sire, hear and judge: there was a rich man who possessed a hundred lambs, and there was a poor man who had only one. The rich man took the sheep and killed the poor man. What must the rich man do?

DAVID: Surely he must give up four sheep.

NATHAN: Sire, you are the rich man, Uriah the poor, and Bethsheba the sheep.

BETHSHEBA: Me, a lamb!

DAVID: Ah! I have sinned! I've sinned, I've sinned.

NATHAN: Good, since you admit it, the Lord's going to transfer your sin; it's indeed enough that Absalom slept with all your wives; marry the beautiful Bethsheba; one of the sons you will have with her will reign over all Israel, and I will name him lovable, and the children of legitimate and honest wives will be massacred.

BETHSHEBA: By Adonai, you are a charming prophet; come here, so I can embrace you!

DAVID: Hey, there, there, easy. Let the prophet be given something to drink; as for the rest of us, let's rejoice, go, since everything's going well I want to compose gallant songs. Let me have my harp! (playing his harp)

Dear Hebrews by heaven sent,
In blood you'll bathe your feet.
And your dogs will grow fat
On the blood they lick.
Have care, my dear friends
Of taking all the little ones;
Still at the breast
You'll crush their skulls,
Against the wall of infidelity.
And your dogs will grow fat
With the blood they lick.

BETHSHEBA: Are these your gallant songs?

DAVID: (singing and dancing)

And your dogs will grow fat
With the blood they lick,

BETHSHEBA: Will you stop your airs of body guard? That's abominable, no savage would want to sing of such horrors. The butcher of the people of Gag and Magag would be ashamed of it.

DAVID: (still leaping around)

And the dogs will grow fat
With the blood they lick,

BETHSHEBA: I'm going away if you continue to sing like this, and hop around like a drunk: you are showing everything that you wear; Fie! What manners!

DAVID: I will dance, I will dance. I will be yet more loathsome, I will dance before servants, I will show all that I am wearing and that will glorify me before young women.

JOAB: Now that you've actually danced you must set your affairs in order.

DAVID: Yes, you are right. There's a time for everything. Let's return to Heru-Chalaim.

JOAB: You shall always have war; you must have some money in reserve, and know how many of your subjects can march in campaign, and how many will remain to cultivate the earth.

DAVID: The advice is very acute: let's go, Bethsheba: we're going to reign my love.

(he dances and sings)

And the dogs will grow fat
From the blood they lick.

CURTAIN

ACT V

HERU-CHALAIM

DAVID: (seated before a table, his officers around him) Six hundred ninety four shillings and half a share, and on the other thirteen hundred and a quarter make eight hundred seven shillings and three quarters. So that's all that was found in my treasury, there's no more of the wherewithal to pay my men one day.

A CLERK OF THE TREASURY: Milord, the times are hard.

DAVID: And they're going to be much more so for you. I need money, you hear?

JOAB: Milord, Your Highness stole like all other kings; the men of the exchequer, the suppliers of the army, pillage all. They make good cheer at our expense, and the soldier dies of hunger.

DAVID: I'll have them cut in two; indeed to-day we had the worst cheer in the world.

JOAB: That doesn't prevent these swindlers charging you every day for your table thirty fat cattle, one hundred fat sheep, as many stags, she-goats, wild boars, thirty barrels of refined flour, and sixty barrels of ordinary flour.

DAVID: Stop, will you, you want to laugh; that would be wherewithal to nourish the whole court of the King of Assyria and all that of the King of the Indies for six months.

JOAB: Nothing is yet more true, for this is written in your books.

DAVID: What! While I lack wherewithal to pay my butcher?

JOAB: It's because they are stealing from Your Royal Highness, as I've already had the honor to tell you.

DAVID: How much cash ought I to have in the hands of my controller-general do you think?

JOAB: Milord, your books declare that you have 800 hundred talents of gold, two million, eighty thousand talents of silver, and 10,000 gold drachmas, which makes at the lowest price of one trillion three hundred twenty million 500 thousand pounds sterling.

DAVID: You are mad, I think; the whole land cannot furnish a quarter of those riches, how could you expect me to have amassed this treasure in such a small country that has not the least commerce?

JOAB: I don't know anything about it; I'm not a financier.

DAVID: You only tell me stupidities like you are; I will know my count however little it may be; and you, Yeses, have you finished enumerating the people?

YESES: Yes, Milord; you have eleven hundred thousand Israeli men, and four hundred seventy thousand from Judah enrolled to march against your enemies.

DAVID: What! I have fifteen hundred seventy thousand men under arms? that's difficult in a country, which at present can nourish only 30,000 souls; at this reckoning by taking one soldier for every ten persons that would make fifteen million seven hundred thousand subjects in my empire: Babylon doesn't have that many.

JOAB: That's the miracle.

DAVID: Ah! I insist on knowing exactly how many subjects I have. They won't increase them on me; I don't believe we are 30,000.

AN OFFICER: Here's your chaplain-ordinary, the Reverend Doctor Gag, who's just come on the part of the Lord to speak to Your Royal Highness.

DAVID: He couldn't pick a worse time, but let him enter.

(Enter Doctor Gag)

DAVID: What do you want, Doctor Gag?

GAG: I've come to tell you that you've committed a great sin.

DAVID: What do you mean? In what, if you please?

GAG: By having your people counted.

DAVID: What do you mean, nut that you are? Is there an operation more wise and more useful than to know the number of his subjects? Isn't a shepherd obliged to count his sheep?

GAG: All that is well and good. But God is giving you the choice of famine or plague.

DAVID: Prophet of misfortune, I intend at least that you may be punished for your fine mission; I would do vainly to choose famine, the rest of you priests always have good cheer; if I choose war you don't go there. I'll choose plague. I hope you catch it, and that you croak the way you deserve.

GAG: God be blessed!

(He runs out screaming "Plague" and every-one shouts "The Plague, the Plague!")

JOAB: I don't understand all this. What! The plague for having reckoned his score?

(Bethsheba enters with Salomon)

BETHSHEBA: Eh, Milord! You must have the devil in you to choose the plague; seventy thousand people died on the spot, and I think I already have anthrax. I am trembling for myself and my son Salomon that I am bringing you.

DAVID: I've got worse than anthrax; I am weary of all this; it's then necessary that I have more plague victims than sub-jects: listen, I'm getting old, you are no longer beautiful, my feet are always cold. I need a girl of fifteen to warm me up.

JOAB: By jingo, Milord, I know one who will do your thing. Her name is Abesag of Sunam.

DAVID: Let her be brought to me, let her be brought to me, let her warm me up.

BETHSHEBA: Truly, you are a villainous debauchee. Fie, at your age. What do you want to do with a little girl?

JOAB: Milord, there she comes. I will present her to you.

DAVID: Come indeed, little girl. Will you actually warm me up?

ABESAG: Wow, Milord, I've really warmed up others.

BETHSHEBA: Now see how you are abandoning me; you don't love me any more! And what will become of my son Salomon to whom you promised your inheritance?

DAVID: Oh! I'll keep my word, he's a little lad who's completely according to my heart; he already loves women like a mad man; approach, little wise-guy so I can embrace you; I'm making you king, you hear?

SALOMON: Milord, I much prefer to reign under you.

DAVID: Now there's a pretty reply; I am very satisfied with him. Go, you will soon reign, my child, for I feel I'm getting feeble; women have ruined my health; but you will have a much more beautiful harem than me.

SALOMON: I hope to derive honor from it.

BETHSHEBA: How witty my son is. I wish he was already on the throne.

(Enter Adonias)

ADONIAS: Father, I'm coming to cast myself at your feet.

DAVID: This kid has never pleased me.

ADONIAS: Father, I have two boons to ask of you; the first is to name me your successor on account of I am the son of a princess and that Salomon is the fruit of an adulterous commerce, to whom the law owes nothing but an alimony pension at most. Don't violate the law of all nations in his favor.

BETHSHEBA: Indeed this little urchin deserves to be defenestrated.

DAVID: You are right. What is the other boon you want, little wretch?

ADONIAS: My Lord, it's the young Abesag of Sunam who is of no use to you; I love her to distraction, and I beg you to give her to me by will.

DAVID: This rogue will make me die of chagrin. I feel myself getting weak, I can't take any more. Warm me up a bit, Abesag.

(Adonias leaves)

ABESAG: (taking his hand) I'm doing what I can, but you are cold as ice.

DAVID: I feel I am dying. Let them place me on my bed of repose.

SALOMON: (throwing himself at his feet) O King! Live a long while.

BETHSHEBA: May he die right now, the villainous leper, and let us reign in peace.

DAVID: My last hour's come. I need to make my will, and forgive, as a good

Jew, all my enemies; Salomon, I am making you Jewish King, remember to be clement and gentle; don't fail, as soon as my eyes are closed to assassinate my son Adonias, even if he were to be embracing the horns of the altar.

SALOMON What wisdom! What beauty of soul! Father, I shall not fail in my word.

DAVID: See this Joab who served me in my wars, and to whom I owe my crown; I beg you in the name of the Lord, to have him assassinated, too for he put blood in my slippers.

JOAB: What! Monster! I will strangle you with my own hands, go, go, I will indeed break your will, and your son Salomon will see what sort of man I am.

SALOMON: Is this all, my dear father? Have you no one else to do away with?

DAVID: I've got a bad memory; hold on, there's a certain Semei who used to tell me certain things. We commend ourselves—I will swear him, by the living God that I will pardon him, that he served me very well, that he is of my privy council; you are wise, don't fail to have him killed as a traitor.

SALOMON: Your will shall be executed, my dear father.

DAVID: Go, you will be the wisest of kings, and the Lord will give you a thousand wives as reward; I am dying! Let me embrace you once more! Goodbye!

BETHSHEBA: God be thanked, we we're getting exhausted

AN OFFICER: Let's quickly go bury ou good King David.

ALL: Our good King David, the model of

princes, the man after the heart of the Lord.

ABESAG: What will become of me? Who will I warm up?

SALOMON: Come here, come here, you will be happier with me than with my good natured father.

CURTAIN

AVIS

Voltaire supposedly adapted and translated this play from the work of a Dutch writer named Huet, although no trace of a drama with this theme or title by Huet is known to exist.

Mr. Huet, member of the English Parliament was the grand-nephew of Mr. Huet, Bishop of Avanches. The English pronounce "Huet" with an open "E" as "Hut." It was he, who, in 1778 composed this very curious little book, *The Man After the Heart of God*. Indignant at having heard a commentator compare David to King George II, who had neither assassinated any one nor burned his French prisoners in a brick oven, he did shining justice to this Jewish knight.

ABOUT FRANK J. MORLOCK

FRANK J. MORLOCK has written and translated many plays since retiring from the legal profession in 1992. His translations have also appeared on Project Gutenberg, the Alexandre Dumas Père web page, Literature in the Age of Napoléon, Infinite Artistries.com, and Munsey's (formerly Blackmask). In 2006 he received an award from the North American Jules Verne Society for his translations of Verne's plays. He lives and works in México.

www.ingramcontent.com/pod-product-compliance
Lightning Source LLC
LaVergne TN
LVHW041206080426
835508LV00008B/821